3 Ingredient C_

A Thirsty
Jane Guide

J.K. O'Hanlon

evenSO Press
Prairie Village, Kansas

Copyright © 2013 J.K. O'Hanlon

Photographs of all drinks, author and photos on pages 7,9,10,13,14,15,17,21,23,95 by Lisarae Turnbull-Oliva copyright © 2012 Lisarae Photo Design.

Although the author and publisher have made every effort to ensure the accuracy and completeness of information contained in this book, we assume no responsibility for errors, inaccuracies, omissions, or any inconsistency herein. Any slights of people, places, or organizations are unintentional.

Any trademarks, service marks, or product names used in this book are assumed to be the property of their respective owners, and are used only for reference. Use of any trademarks, service marks or product names does not imply that this book is authorized by, affiliated with, or in any way endorsed by the owners of such trademarks, service marks, or products.

Library of Congress Control Number: 2012948108

ISBN 978-0-988-27391-7

Printed in the United States of America

First Edition

Book Design by Kim Mann, Mann Made Design Incorporated

Quantity discounts are available on bulk purchases of this book. For information, contact evenSO Press, LLC, 3965 West 83rd Street #267, Prairie Village, KS 66208. www.evensopress.com

3 Ingredient Cocktails

for
Paul

Table of Contents

Intro to Boozing 101

It's Just a Cocktail, Yet So Much More

Thirsty Jane Maxim No. 1: With only three ingredients to wrangle, anyone can make a great cocktail without stress and without going broke.

As easy as it should be, so many people balk at diving into the exciting, delicious and sexy cocktail culture that inundates our society. Why? The story I've gotten from most friends is similar to an experience from my own home bar. One day, I asked my man to make me a cocktail. His eyes got round and beads of sweat pearled on his forehead. Here was one of the most competent human beings I've ever known stressed out at the thought of making a drink! I assured him he'd be able to find something simple in one of the several dozen recipe books on the shelf by the bar. Thirty minutes later he came up from the bar empty handed and frustrated.

> Would you be a dear and make me a cocktail?

> Oh, shit.

The gist of his explanation: It was too hard. There were too many recipes to choose from. Too many esoteric ingredients. And he wasn't sure he could substitute a gin for the one specified in the recipe without ruining the drink. Perhaps the new mixology has become so complex in a quest for authenticity and innovation that, for the average Thirsty Jane or Joe making a drink is intimidating and confusing, and requires hundreds of dollars in obscure liquors. Thirsty Jane is here to roll in the booze cart, start shaking and de-mystify mixology.

The time has come for home bars to reclaim the great American cocktail.

Oh Say Can You Swill?

The cocktail is the quintessential American drink. Other cultures mixed drinks for hundreds of years before the U.S. existed. One of the early examples of a mixed drink is punch. In the American Colonies, massive bowls of punch kept the founding fathers lubricated in between altering the balance of power in the world and tending to their farms or law practices. By punch, I do not refer to that sickeningly sweet bright pink frothy mixture at your cousin Barry's wedding reception that looked like it could actually take shape and crawl out of the bowl. Punch in Colonial days typically meant rum, brandy, water and a "shrub" (a mixture of sugar, lemon peel and juice; not a bush or tree of any sort). The stuff is deceptively boozy. Not to mention seriously yummy.

Although the recipe for punch looks a lot like what we call a cocktail today, it wasn't until the early 1800s that the term "cocktail" was used, and it was not in connection with punch. In 1806, the term "cock tail" appeared in a New York newspaper in connection with the bill of fare for a politician. In response to a reader's query about the term "cock tail," the newspaper clarified that it was "a stimulating liquor, composed of spirits of any kind, sugar water, and bitters…."

The origin of the name remains a mystery. Some say that because it was a morning drink, its name came from a rooster's wake-up call. Another legend attributes the word cocktail to a bastardization of the French word "coquetier," a type of cup used in New Orleans in the 1800s to serve mixed drinks. Probably another dozen tales exist to explain how a mixed drink came to be known

by this odd name. Regardless of how it got its name, a cocktail was only one type of drink. For example, in one of the earliest books on bartending, cocktails comprised only 10 of the nearly 450 recipes. Other categories included punches, flips, fizzes, slings, juleps, cobblers and more. Because of the cocktail's simplicity (surprise — usually just three or four ingredients), its popularity took off.

Red, White and Booze

It was during Prohibition, though, that Americans elevated the cocktail to an art form. Folks with money could buy quality booze smuggled in by bootleggers, head off shore on luxury boats into international waters where booze was legal, or even travel to Havana for a daiquiri or Cuba Libre. The rest of the schmucks got by with really bad

booze. The worst of it killed you; the best of it required serious doctoring to make it palatable. The cocktail provided an excellent way to mask the taste of bathtub gin.

Alcohol production diminished during World War II as industry focused on the war effort and rationing went into effect. After the war, however, life was good. Very good. Distillers responded to Americans' demand for booze by pushing blended whiskeys and neutral grain spirits (like gin and vodka) that did not require aging. The 1950s were the cocktail's zenith. Whether it was Dad's three-martini lunch or Mom's double highball at a bridge party, an entire generation grew up watching their parents imbibe booze.

So, of course, when that generation reached drinking age, it rejected hard liquor and turned to illegal drugs as the inebriant of choice. The 1970s were almost as bleak. Grain neutral spirits with sweet, fruity mixes were the norm if someone was going to order a mixed drink. More people turned to wine, which was gaining momentum in California at the time.

By the 1980s, the prestige of single-malt scotches took hold for the next generation, those who made "keeping up with the Joneses" a competitive sport. American bourbon producers followed suit to produce superb single-batch and single-barrel whiskeys. As drinkers appreciated the fine taste of Scotch and American whiskeys, the cocktail began to experience a resurrection.

This resurgence might be partially attributed to a new generation's desire to differentiate itself from its wine-swilling parents. However, a major appeal to hard liquor over wine is the value per drink: a $20 bottle of vodka yields approximately 12 drinks, while a $20 bottle of wine will give you only about four. Additionally, in America, it is always a matter a time before the "old" is the "new." The current vein of nostalgia running through our society for the speakeasy culture has revived interest in vintage cocktails and the spirits with which they are made.

Cocktails are hip again. So when I wanted to find a book for my guy, I thought surely there would be something out there. Maybe something crazy easy with three ingredients, like one of those cook-books on the shelf we use for quickie dinners? Determined to find a solution for him, I searched the Internet in vain for a truly simple drink book. I found hundreds of three-ingredient books for dinner, but nothing like that for a drink. Apparently it is easier to make dinner than a freaking cocktail! That, my thirsty friends, is simply un-American.

To remedy the dearth of basic cocktailing knowledge, I started com-piling simple and tasty recipes — all with three ingredients or less — for friends and family. They clamored for more and began mixing on their own to great success. Finally, my honey convinced me that others would benefit from my perspective that everyone can make a good drink without stressing out or bleeding their bank accounts.

Just Mix it
Let's be clear. I'm not a professional bartender. I'm not affiliated with the spirits industry in any way (other than being a consistent revenue source for them). I am merely Thirsty Jane, an average chick in search of a great quick drink. I also love everything else about cocktails, from the history of a spirit, to wacky anecdotes about the origin of a drink, to groovy vintage glassware, to the colors and aromas of a spectacular drink. Most of all, I love mixing it up for my friends. My passion is to find the perfect drink for someone or craft the ultimate cocktail for a party.

This book is not written for the professionals or even the über-serious jigger jockeys out there. There are hundreds of amazing books with thousands of recipes and thousands of pages of detailed information to satisfy those individuals' quest for knowledge. This book is for the average person who is new to cocktails and would like to learn to mix at home or be more knowledgeable when ordering at a bar. Further-more, if you already enjoy cocktails but have been too intimidated to try them at home, experimenting with these recipes will give you the skills needed to mix with confidence.

The recipes in this book are mostly classic cocktails with a few after dinner drinks and some more modern takes on vintage favor-ites. Not every recipe in this book will please every person, of course. Although I must admit, I love them all! You might want to start with one particular spirit and try out a couple or all of the recipes in that category. Each type of booze is labeled on the right side of the page with the same color. You'll also find a symbol at the bottom to show what kind of drink it is. This allows you to shuffle through the pages and pick a few that might fit the mood, season or occasion before you.

This leads to Thirsty Jane Maxim No. 2: You can't make a great cocktail without making a few duds.

God and my friends know I've had more than my share of drinks that have gone down the drain. Literally. Here's your license to try something new. Experiment. A cocktail is too important to be taken seriously. So have fun mixing, shaking and stirring. Let me know how it goes, too. What did you like or not like? What do you want more of from Thirsty Jane's Guides? Do you have a favorite three-ingredient recipe you'd like to share? Visit www.thirstyjane.com to share your stories and find out what else is getting mixed up at my bar!

This revolution in cocktails is not reserved for master mixologists or liquor industry experts. It is your cocktail hour. So get your jigger ready, your ice cubes prepared, and your liquor primed. No one should leave your bar thirsty!

Tools of the Trade

Cocktails are sexy. The boozy smells and tastes, shapely shakers, groovy glasses, colorful garnishes and sleek stainless steel gadgets scream hipness. Being a part of this resurgent culture is fashionable and cool, so you want to have all of the right stuff when you get ready to shake it up for some friends on a Friday night. But, you also need to pay the bills, so investing in the perfect shaker and every type of glass and super-premium liquor may not be in the cards at this moment.

Fear not.

Thirsty Jane Maxim No. 3: Never let the lack of the right gizmos get in the way of mixing a drink. Never. Ever.

Do not be deterred in your quest for a martini even if the only glass-ware available is your best friend's three-year old's tippy cup. Just

wash that bad boy up and make do. Necessity is the mother of invention, and the history of almost every booze is proof of that saying.

But let's say you want to take it up a notch and stock your bar, then the following should get you to a pretty impressive place without breaking the bank.

Glassware

The majority of drinks are served in one of three types of glasses: The highball glass is a tall thin glass usually around 10 to 12 ounces. There are plenty of these types of glasses in discount stores. Just avoid the really big pint glasses or your drinks with be alternatively super boozy or really wimpy.

The double old-fashioned or rocks glass is short and squat and can be anywhere from 6 to 12 ounces. You can find some really groovy

retro rocks glasses in thrift stores or the basement of your dead great aunt. I'm not trying to be morose; she would want you to be enjoying those glasses. Trust me.

A cocktail glass can be the V-shaped martini glass, which emanates "swank" for a martini or Manhattan. You may also consider a coupe glass which you see featured in many of the photos in this book. It looks a little like what the old saucer shaped champagne glasses look like. I once scored 4 of these uber-groovy-retro ones for $6 at a thrift store. Use one of these for a retro cocktail and people with think you've gone semi-pro in mixology.

You will also see a few other specialty glasses in the photos in this book. A few champagne flutes are a good investment because you will be celebrating something at some point. Some shot glasses are also good to have around. Once you get skilled at pouring those layered shots, you'll want to show them off. Again, check out discount retailers and clearance centers for these types of glasses. Unless you are planning a big party, probably 4 of each type is a good place to start. One mixologist friend has very few matching glasses. He loves to give everyone their own unique glass at a party. Most of his vintage bar ware come from estate sales and thrift stores.

Gadgets

Personally, I'd rather score some hip glasses and scrimp on the gadgets, and I am a techno-geek extraordinaire. That said, the most important gadget is a cocktail shaker. There are two styles. The cobbler shaker is the iconic three-piece set you see at most stores and in illustrations relating to martinis. People love giving me these. Here's the deal: the top gets stuck on frequently and you end up looking very uncool banging that sucker in your sink to get the top off. Then, the baby pops off and ricochets out of the sink all over your best friend's white sequined tank top. And you just mixed something blue. Not good. If you watch most bartenders, they use a Boston shaker which is basically the bottom part of a cobbler shaker with a pint glass on the top. You put the pint glass in at a bit of an angle and tap it down pretty aggressively. Hold on tight and shake like there's no tomorrow.

A little knock to the side of the pint glass usually breaks the seal. Use a strainer to strain your drink. When you are at the vacation rental place without any bar tools, just find two glasses which fit together and open up the edge to strain your drink. Or use a fork to strain. Just make the damned drink!

I measure booze like I measure stuff when I cook. A little of this, a little of that. Flavor to taste. After a while, you get the feel for what an ounce is, and if you're a little off, well, so be it. But, when you first start mixing, I recommend getting a jigger. There are plenty of kinds out there. One of my favorites has always been a $1.50 plastic special which is divided on one side into 1, 2, and 3 oz. and on the other size by .50, .75 and 1.5 oz.

Fresh juice is essential to a great drink, so plan on investing in some sort of juicing apparatus unless you have hands of steal. You can get a reamer, a standard juicer, a hand juicer which is kind of a clamp thing, or if you know you are going to be making 50 margaritas (yes, that means you are going to be squeezing a minimum of 25 limes) an electric juicer for about $20 (not the kind you make health drink juices from).

The rest of these gadgets are strictly optional. I just bought my first cocktail spoon after mixing for more years than I want to admit in print. It holds about a teaspoon which means when you double it you get about .25 oz. It's cool, but I have spoons in my house, so why waste money on a spoon when I could be saving up for a different bottle of gin?

The other cool gadget I recently got was a channel knife. The one I got gives me zest, and both wide and skinny lemon or lime peels. It's so much chicer than using a vegetable peeler, but that works just fine, too. You can cut a big peel with a veggie peeler, then use a paring knife to make the skinny twists. Train your twist to go curly by wrapping it around a pencil or your finger, as long as they are clean.

The last handy gadget is a muddler. For years, okay, decades, I just used a wooden spoon. It got the job done and saved me enough money to buy another bottle of rum. It's cool though. There are wooden ones and new fangled stainless ones with rubber tips to really mash that stuff up.

I hope you are getting the point: don't get caught up with having knick knack tools. Use your hard-earned money to get good booze because that my friends is where the real action is.

Booze

Selecting booze is a little like picking a lawyer or buying diapers: get the cheapest that gets the job done. I don't mean use bad stuff, but don't buy a $75 bottle of single malt scotch for a high ball. Don't get an anejo tequila for a margarita. Don't start with the super-premium vodkas if you're mixing with lemonade. But, if you are making a martini, please, I beg you, get a nice bottle of gin because that is what you are going to taste and bad gin is truly bad.

Start your collection with stuff you like to drink. If you know you like vodka, get that first. If you are very new to cocktails, you might want to work your way through this book, learning about the different spirits and buy a bottle for the recipes in each chapter. Buy small bottles in case you find out you really don't like a particular spirit. Even buying a full 750 ml bottle, you should expect to pay less than $20 for pretty decent quality. A basic bar will have one bottle of each of the following:

- English dry gin
- Vodka
- 100 % Blue agave silver tequila
- Silver rum
- Blended scotch

- Bourbon
- Orange flavored liquor (like triple sec, Cointreau or Gran Marnier)
- Coffee flavored liquor (like Kahlua)

To make all of the recipes in this book, you will need to add a few specialty liquors to your bar. Several of the ones on this list are excellent on the rocks as an after dinner drink. Think of which recipes you are interested in making and buy ingredients for a few of them. I would suggest in order of importance a small bottle of:

- Cognac
- Amaretto
- Irish cream liquor (like Bailey's)
- Blue curacao
- Crème de cacao
- Champagne
- Crème de cassis
- White chocolate liquer (like Godiva's)
- Applejack brandy
- Ruby port
- Drambuie
- Galliano
- Campari

Mixes

Small bottles of mixes may be a little more expensive, but unless you are planning on mixing dozens of one kind of drink, you'll end up wasting a lot and taking up a lot of space with big bottles of mixes. Having the following on hand will ensure you can make any of the drinks in this book. Again, I've ordered them from most important to less important:

- Limes for juicing
- Lemons for juicing
- Dry vermouth
- Sweet vermouth
- Angostura bitters
- Tonic water
- Club soda
- Cola
- Ginger ale
- Lemon lime soda
- Grapefruit soda
- Ginger beer (spicier than ginger ale, so get if you can find it; available at most grocery stores; use ginger ale if desperate)
- Bloody Mary mix
- Half and half /cream/milk (according to taste and cholesterol level)

- Simple syrup (buy or make your own by boiling equal parts sugar and water until dissolved)
- Grenadine (sadly, most of the commercial stuff is just colored high fructose corn syrup; make your own using equal parts pomegranate juice and sugar, boiling until syrupy, then cooled)
- Pineapple juice
- Grapefruit juice
- Cranberry juice
- Orange juice

- Rose's lime juice
- Lemonade
- Cream of coconut (loaded with fat and sugar and essential to a great pina colada)

Garnishes

Garnishes are not only glamorous, but also important to a drink. They affect three important senses: sight, smell and taste. A well prepared garnish gives your cocktail that extra flourish as far as presentation, so take your time to prepare a good looking lemon or lime twist or pick out a really well-shaped cherry for a special someone's drink. Because a garnish will change the flavor of a drink through your sense of smell and taste, do not toss citrus peels into a drink willy-nilly. A drink may only need a little lemon over the edge to give the right sense of citrus without getting bitter. All that said, do not let preparing a perfect garnish get in the way of your drink. I've enjoyed many martinis without an olive or twist simply because I'd run out and a trip to the store was out of the question. If you are having a big party, prepare some common garnishes ahead of time and have them available in small dishes at your bar so you don't have to spend too much time cutting lemons and not socializing. If I'm serving margaritas, I'll salt the rims ahead of time. To rim a glass, run a wedge of lime or lemon around the rim or dip the edge of the glass in some simple syrup. Dip your glass in your rimming material and shake off any excess.

Techniques

Practice makes perfect. The more you mix, the more comfortable you will get with straying from recipes and putting your own sense of style into a drink. Making a cocktail in a double old-fashioned glass or highball glass is fairly self-explanatory: add all of the ingredients with a lot of ice and stir. When making a drink to be strained into a cocktail glass, you will need to decide whether to shake or stir. I prefer my drinks very cold, so usually I shake. And, boy, do I shake. By some freakish chance of nature, my hands tolerate a cold shaker better than most normal humans. So, cold means really cold for me. I like seeing the little ice crystals on top of my martini, but not everyone likes that. Some might argue that it is inappropriate to drink a martini like that.

Thirsty Jane vehemently believes that all rules are meant to be broken. So, here's the general rule, and feel free to break it: you should stir gently any drink which is all booze, for example a martini or a Manhatten, but you should shake a drink which has fruit juice or cream or other non-booze item in it so that all of the liquids gets incorporated into each other. Following this technique will yield a clearer cocktail for the stirred versions. When you use juice, clarity is not an issue, so shake.

I've never fussed with differences between ice cubes, big versus small, or whole versus cracked. After consulting numerous authorities, I can't find a definitive answer and actually have found several conflicting pieces of advice. I like smaller cubes or cracked ice for shaking, but if only the big cubes are around, I use those. For a beginner, use cubes from your ice maker or ice cube trays or the bag from the store. If you are throwing a fancy party and are serving drinks in highball or double old-fashioned glasses, consider making some jumbo cubes in square silicone cube makers.

Finger Food

Having some food available while you cocktail is essential. There are plenty of recipes available in cookbooks and on the internet which are simple. I always have on hand a couple of great items such as mixed nuts and other fun party mixes. Also, one appetizer has never failed me: meatballs in BBQ sauce. I keep a bag of meatballs in my freezer and a bottle of BBQ sauce in the pantry. In 10 minutes you have something to give any unexpected guest. Granted, this is not the most glamorous appetizer, but not once has a meatball gone un-eaten. Another quickie and popular item is frozen toasted ravioli with some marinara sauce on the side. Again, not swanky, but inexpensive, storable in your freezer, and always a crowd-pleaser.

Responsible Cocktailing

Thirsty Jane is all about enjoying cocktails respon-sibly. One of the difficult things about cocktails is that you never know exactly how much booze you are getting in a drink. For this reason, you must be extra careful about imbibing especially if you or guests will be driving. Agree on a designat-ed driver before you go to a party. Drink lots of water and eat food. My best piece of advice for avoiding a hangover comes from a very old school bartending book: If you think you can have one more drink, it is time to stop. You will regret "one more" in the morning. Be careful out there, my friends. We don't want to spoil an otherwise good evening.

Gin

The Tonic for Whatever Ails You

A friend once harangued me on a regular basis to name the three albums I'd pick if deserted on an island. Endless variations on the theme plagued me. Three rock albums. Three alternative rock albums. Three bootleg songs. Why couldn't he have asked me for my three favorite cocktails or three favorite boozes? Now, those are questions I could have answered.

Alas, while Thirsty Jane prides herself in being booze inclusive, gin is what's on my deserted tropical island. Clear and cold, it mixes well in a warm weather cocktail, yet can provide the necessary warmth when the cool ocean breezes set in. Plus, a daily gin and tonic theoretically functions as a malaria prophylactic for this walking all-you-can-suck mosquito buffet. Most importantly, gin's Cinderella story tugs at my heart. To rise from the docks to the throne room, then back down to the gutter and up again to the boardroom testifies to gin's tenacity and versatility, qualities Thirsty Jane esteems.

Meet the Gins (and Genevers)

Before we launch into the roller-coaster history of gin, here's a short introduction to what comprises this angelically demonic beverage. Gin begins its journey with a grain mash, much like whiskey. The type of grain varies with the gin. London dry gin, which is not exclusive to London or even England, typically contains 75 percent corn and 25 percent barley. An exception to the corn and barley mix of London dry gin is Plymouth gin, which consists solely of wheat. The first distillation is at very high proof (around 180 to 190) resulting in a clear, crisp and dry alcohol. The neutral spirit is then diluted to around 120 proof before the next distillation.

A second distillation with juniper berries infuses the typical evergreen aromatic. During the second distillation, other flavorings, such as orange or lemon peel, or cardamom, anise, licorice or coriander creates the unique taste of each gin. Premium gins often go through additional distillations to purify the spirit. Many distillers have utilized the same recipes for hundreds of years while keeping the exact ingredients and proportions secret.

Holland gin (also known as Dutch gin or genever) starts with a "malt wine" mixture of barley, corn and rye and is distilled at a low proof. Like London dry gin, genever also goes through a second distillation, infusing the botanicals into the malt wine. The genever comes off that second distillation at a low proof and ages in casks. The result is a very different drink than London dry gin. The pale amber colored liquor not only has the distinct juniper and botanical essence of gin, but also emanates a deep malt reminiscent of a whiskey. Some argue that because of this robust flavor, genever is not appropriate for mixing in a cocktail and should only be drunk straight (neat). I beg to differ. Some very tasty vintage cocktails were crafted with genever. Because it is not widely available outside of Holland and Argentina, and is not a staple of the basic home bar, this book does not include any recipes with genever. Stay tuned, though, because genever is a delightfully complex spirit deserving of attention.

Gyrating Through the Centuries

Speaking of genever, the Dutch deserve a toast for bringing this delightful drink, the precursor to gin, into existence back in the mid 1600s. Physician Franciscus de le Boë Sylvius looked to the juniper berry's diuretic powers to cure stomach and kidney ailments. Fortunately for gin lovers, Dr. Sylvius mixed the juniper berry tonic with a neutral alcohol to make the medicine more palatable. He named his creation "genever" based upon the French word juniper, genièvre. Voila! Gin (the Brits' shortened version of "genever") was born!

Soon, the entire country developed a case of the "bad humors" requiring treatment with Dr. Sylvius' concoction. Commercial production ensued to keep up with the country's demand for the new aromatic spirit. It didn't take long for English soldiers to discover the "Dutch courage" and import it to England. The English version did not mimic the Dutch genever, however. London dry gin incorporated the juniper essence, but not the malt flavor of genever. Additionally, because of the differences in grains and aging, London gin is a colorless, crisp, dry spirit. The popularity of this new drink spread rapidly to become the masses' choice. When Dutchman William of Orange began his reign in 1689, gin found its way out of the seaports and into the royal courts.

Over the next four decades, Parliament enacted a series of laws promoting the distillation and consumption of gin. First, anyone was allowed to distill spirits using English corn in oversupply at the time. Farmers sold their grain, entrepreneurs opened stills and sold gin, and the masses obtained gin easily and cheaply. With high taxes on beer and French brandies, gin became the craze.

The mania quickly turned into an epidemic. Londoners over-served themselves with abandon. Critics claimed the extreme boozing led to an increase in crime, not to mention the decline of moral standards exhibited by (gasp!) women drinking in public.

By 1729, the English government reversed course, ending its enabling of production and consumption of gin by restricting the sale of gin. Surprise, surprise — the masses ignored the laws and continued to illegally produce and sell gin. The drunken debauchery continued. In 1733, Parliament surrendered and again endorsed the liberal production and sale of gin. As the French might say, "Laissez les bon temp rouler!" The masses partied on, but bad press for Mother Gin gained momentum.

Between 1736 and 1750, a new series of laws reined in gin's dominion. Taxes and strict licensing, followed by a corn crop a failure, made gin inaccessible to the lower classes. The upper class, which could still afford the spirit, demanded quality. With the invention of the column still in the 1830s, the first premium English gin became available. Early distillers included Tanqueray, Gordon's, Boodles, Booth's, Beefeater, and Gilbey's, all names still familiar at the local liquor store. Glitzy "gin palaces" catering to the upper class sprang up around London.

Gin then began its world-wide tour of intoxication courtesy of the British Empire. In tropical areas, colonists cut the bitter taste of quinine (used to combat malaria) with gin. I raise my glass to my familiar foe, the mosquito, in celebration of the drink of summer, the gin and tonic. Hurrah! This delightful summer concoction made its way back to the mother country where ladies enjoyed it at afternoon tea parties. Less than 200 years into its existence, gin cycled from a lowly drink to royal courts, back to the gutter and up again to a highfalutin drink.

Gutter-snipe gin did not disappear forever, however. In 1919, the temperance movement in America succeeded in getting the Volstead Act passed, and the Prohibition era began. Like England's attempts to curtail the drinking of gin, Prohibition could not stop alcohol consumption and only drove it underground into a world of organized crime. During Prohibition, gin became the drink of choice in speakeasies because of its production simplicity—juniper and other flavorings steeped for a week in a bathtub with any potable alcohol (sadly, some of the stuff used was lethal). For thirteen years, gin maintained a clandestine reign in the United States. The wealthy could afford quality imports from England obtained through bootleggers, and the rest of America's gin drinkers turned to the bathtub moonshiners.

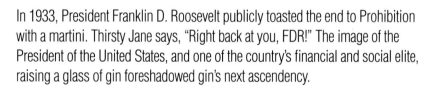

In 1933, President Franklin D. Roosevelt publicly toasted the end to Prohibition with a martini. Thirsty Jane says, "Right back at you, FDR!" The image of the President of the United States, and one of the country's financial and social elite, raising a glass of gin foreshadowed gin's next ascendency.

The Great Depression echoed England's tough times in the 1700s, driving people to alcohol in order to soften the suffering. The great American cocktail gained popularity, a product of Prohibition days when mixing juices and liquors made the bathtub booze palatable. Hollywood made drinking cocktails like the gin martini sexy. And, when Hollywood jumps, the American populace jumps higher, or at least it tries. By the end of World War II, prosperity returned and the middle class emulated the upper class vogue. Cocktail hour and the three-martini lunch became de rigueur, with gin holding court.

Gin's gyration was not over yet. In the 1960s and 1970s, the use of recreational drugs proliferated and replaced alcohol as the gateway to relaxation. When cocktails began a resurgence in the 1990s—thank you again, Hollywood—vodka pushed gin aside as the most popular spirit, even replacing gin in a classic martini. Like all great Cinderella stories, just when you think she is down for the count and give up hope on Mother Gin, she bounces back. Super-premium gins and nostalgia for cocktails of the speakeasy culture have sparked renewed interest in gin. Given gin's resilience, she will probably be back and on top before long.

For G&T Virgins:
Fill a highball glass with ice, add in a shot glass or so of gin (1 ½ to 3 ounces, depending on how boozy you are feeling and big your glass is), fill the rest of the glass with tonic water, and squeeze in a little lime. Cheers!

Way Better Than You Remember

Most people who tell me they don't like gin have either never had gin or have had bad gin in inappropriate quantities and combinations, usually in college. A number of non-gin drinkers reacted favorably to the gin cocktails in this chapter. Most surprising was the number of these gin antagonist drinkers who described the classic martini, which is quite a boozy drink, as smooth. Thirsty Jane wishes she could credit her mixologist skills to the conversion of her taste testers, but honestly, the gin deserves the credit.

Although Plymouth and Hendricks are two of my favorite gins, when mixing for a crowd I'm eager to save a few bucks and go for a more value-oriented, yet still quality, gin. There are plenty to choose from at your local liquor store. A few names include Beefeater, Bombay, Boodles, and Tanqueray. Take a little sip and let it roll around your mouth before you swallow. A good gin brings forth sensations of smoothness and warmth with a hint of floral and does not burn when swallowed. A good dry gin will also finish clean, meaning the taste should not linger in your mouth for long.

Now You're Ready for Another

So, when a case of the "bad humors" brings you down, or an irrational fear of contracting malaria sets in, reach for Dr. Sylvius' invention and relax. Cheers!

Gin Gimlet

3 ounces gin
1 ½ ounces Rose's lime juice

Combine with ice in a cocktail shaker.
Shake and strain into cocktail glass.
Garnish with a thin slice of lime if desired.

What's a Gimlet?
Why, of course,
it's a small tool
for drilling
tiny holes. This drink
was named for the
"penetrating" effects it
has on a drinker.

The Barstool Buzz:

"Refreshing."

"Outstanding balance of booze and citrus."

"Looks like a lot of lime, but I love it."

Thirsty Jane Martini

2 ½ ounces gin
½ ounce dry vermouth
olive or lemon twist

Combine with ice in a cocktail shaker.
Shake and strain into cocktail glass.
Garnish with olive or lemon twist.

The origin of the martini is surprisingly shadowy. Some attribute its creation to "Professor" Jerry Thomas, the author of what many consider to be the first cocktail recipe book. However, the first published recipe for a martini didn't appear until 1882 in a book by New York bartender Harry Johnson.

The Barstool Buzz:

"A classic."

"Crisp and refreshing."

"Smooooooooooth, but with a kick."

Bronx Variation

2 ounces gin
1 ounce orange juice
1 ounce sweet vermouth

Combine with ice in a cocktail shaker.
Shake and strain into cocktail glass.
Garnish with an orange twist if desired.

A Waldorf-Astoria
patron challenged the
bartender to create
something new.
Next thing they knew,
the bar was blowing
through a case of oranges
a day to meet demand
for this popular variation
on the classic martini.

The Barstool Buzz:

"Perfect for breakfast."

"Floats on the tongue."

"Sunday morning delight."

Negroni

1 ounce gin
1 ounce Campari
1 ounce sweet vermouth

Combine with ice in a cocktail shaker.
Shake and strain into cocktail glass.
Garnish with a lemon twist if desired.

**Quintessential
Summer Cocktail**

Another Prohibition
era drink, the Negroni
hails from Italy where
the bitter Campari
is made. Definitely an
acquired taste, once
Campari captivates
your palate, there's
no going back.
Kind of like summer.

The Barstool Buzz:

"Lusty, voluptuous and satisfying."

"Pretty and wicked."

"Delightfully bittersweet, like a boy's first love."

White Lady

1 ½ ounces gin
¾ ounce orange liqueur
½ ounce lemon juice

Combine with ice in a cocktail shaker.
Shake and strain into cocktail glass.
Garnish with a lemon twist if desired.

Born during Prohibition
at Harry's Bar in Paris
where "Lost Generation"
writers like Hemingway
frequently imbibed.
Thirsty Jane uses slightly
less juice than in the
original recipe —
too tart for this
generation's palate!

The Barstool Buzz:

"An anytime drink."

"Citrusy-wow."

"A way to end the summer."

Vodka

The Many Facets of the 'Flavorless' Spirit

What happens if you ask a Pole or a Russian who invented vodka? Hands flail. Faces redden. Voices boom. Blood pressures rise. Guts clench. Tempers flare. That's passion. The same thing happens when you ask a serious mixologist for a vodka and lemonade. Something incredibly important has to be going on to get people's panties in such a wad!

The vodka-belt heavyweights can debate until the cows come home about which country can claim vodka as its invention. And the professional cocktail crafters can stand on soapboxes and beat their chests about the inferiority of the neutral spirit vodka. There's probably truth in everyone's claims. But the bottom line is that vodka is king. It dominates the spirits industry and evokes passion as pure and clear as the spirit itself. That, my thirsty friends, is sexy and irresistible. You can fight it, or you can get on the bus and have a good time.

Something in the Water

Technically, U.S. Treasury Department regulations define vodka as being without character, aroma or taste. Why, then, do hundreds of brands clutter the liquor store shelves, with more entering the marketplace every year? Some say it's about the water. The Russian and Polish words for water are, respectively, "voda" and "woda". "Vodka" is nothing more than a cutesy way to talk about water and can be translated as "dear little water."

Premium distillers often point to the unique qualities of their sour water, such as artesian wells, glaciers, or ice-cold Siberian lake water as the distinguishing factors in their vodka. Although a variety of organic matter can be the base for vodka, the multiple distillations and charcoal filtrations remove the flavorings these ingredients would have imparted into the alcohol. Water seems like the logical choice for what makes one brand different than its comrade on the shelf.

Or is it that simple? The process of making vodka is straightforward. A mash is made of any vegetal material. Grain, specifically rye and wheat, is the most common base, but potatoes, grapes, molasses and corn are also used.

The high-end Eastern and Northern European exports typically are rye- or wheat-based. The Poles have become famous, rightly so, for their smooth as a baby's bottom potato vodka. Whatever mash is used, it is fermented, then distilled multiple times, usually in a column still. The end product is filtered through charcoal to remove any impurities, leaving a very clean spirit.

The "flavorless" spirit lends itself to limitless infusions. The shelves are blanketed with different flavors, from the sedate vanilla or lemon to the curious bacon or wasabi. With more than 100 varieties available, flavored vodka comprises over a fourth of all vodka sales. These products are fun and allow for infinite drink options. Think before you buy, though. That bottle of vanilla vodka bought several years ago for some clever themed drink at a party is collecting dust on my bar. So buy small unless you are having a whopping big party and plan on pushing that specialty cocktail like last year's fad on the closeout rack.

Flavored vodka invokes its share of negative energy among well-heeled mixologists, but it has one of the oldest and most prestigious pedigrees in the booze universe. Russians flavored vodka as early as the 15th century, but the aristocracy took it to a new level during the reign of Catherine the Great in the late 1700s. Using premium ingredients, Russian elites triple-distilled vodka and added flavorings on a fourth distillation. Although the number of flavors wasn't close to today's standards, there were dozens of options ranging from spices to herbals to fruits. On your next trip to Poland, try Zubrowka — bison grass vodka — traditionally served neat with a side of apple juice. Yummy! After we break out the flavored vodkas from Poland at my bar, there's a 50-50 chance Thirsty Jane will appear in full-blown Polish folk costume including, but not limited to, the sequined and tasseled black velvet vest and flowered headdress. Yes, the stuff is that good!

Power to the People

Vodka's intoxicating history reaches back so far that no one is exactly sure of its origins. In Poland, aficionados look to the eighth century when Poles "distilled" spirits by leaving fermented wine out to freeze, then sloughing off the frozen water to get a concentrated spirit. The alcohol initially was used medicinally, but by the 1400s Poles began imbibing the stuff for pure enjoyment, or perhaps more likely as a diversion from the cold and difficult times.

Russia stakes its claim to vodka based upon spirits created by monks in the 12th or 13th century. The monks probably learned early distillation techniques from their Italian counterparts who picked up the practices from travelers from Arabia. Although the exact origins are nebulous, by 1500 vodka was being produced in Russia and drunk prodigiously by the peasantry to celebrate everything from births to weddings to funerals.

As the power of vodka captured the peasants' hearts, souls and bodies, aristocracies in both Russia and Poland noted the industry's profit potential and attempted to seize control of the spirit's production and sale, as a way to control the purses of the underclass. Like Americans would learn hundreds of years later, when it comes to booze, where there's a will, there's a way. So for a good part of the late 1500s through the mid-1700s, the pendulum swung back and forth between state control and peasant revolt.

By the late 1700s, Catherine the Great controlled production of vodka in Russia, and Poland ceased to exist after being partitioned several times and divided amongst Russia, Prussia and Austria. Poland's people never lost their identity or their quest to produce fine vodkas, though. Production innovations included the charcoal filtration system in the 1860s, which was first used by a Russian distiller named Smirnov. (Does that name sound familiar?) Charcoal filtration removes congeners, the organic elements from the base grain or fruit, which give flavor to the alcohol. There are thousands of congener types, and depending on the type of spirit being produced, a distiller will want some to remain in order to give the alcohol a unique flavor. But not with vodka.

With technological advances, the Russian aristocratic landowners produced better and better quality booze. People sucked it down. And tax revenues soared. Eventually, however, peasants rebelled against the onerous rules that confined sales to state-controlled stores. Bootlegging became rampant. Tensions continued to mount between the classes until revolution erupted in 1917. One very wealthy distiller, the aforementioned Vladimir Smirnov, managed to escape the terror and chaos by fleeing to Paris.

The Switzerland of Spirits

Until Smirnov's arrival in France, vodka was a regional drink of Russia, Poland and the Scandinavian countries. The nexus between vodka's rise to stardom and the popularity of cocktails is natural. As a neutral spirit, vodka mixes easily with so many juices and other liquors. The 1920s cocktail craze gave rise to one of the most popular vodka drinks of all time: the Bloody Mary. Invented in Paris' Ritz Hotel, the Bloody Mary became de rigueur for hangovers of the party-hearty Europeans and ex-pats. Before long, the Bloody Mary crossed the Atlantic, got spiced up, and became popular in New York.

Americans were still predominately whiskey drinkers until after World War II. Other spirits invaded whiskey's sacred ground. Sailors stationed in the Caribbean brought back their tastes for rum. The martini was swanky. The darling drink made with tequila, the margarita, was taking Hollywood by storm. The door opened for vodka, and an enterprising Los Angeles bar owner and the new owner of the Smirnov label, renamed "Smirnoff," concocted the Moscow Mule. Simple, but with a kick, the Moscow Mule is lime juice, ginger beer and vodka, served traditionally in a copper mug. Any highball glass will do, mind you!

(Never let the lack of the "perfect" glass get in your way of enjoying a good drink.)

Hollywood legends kept their engraved mugs at the bars. Vodka became the "in" drink of the stars. Soon the rest of the country followed like lemmings running off the cliff. The neutral spirit, vodka, took off and benefited from Smirnoff's brilliant marketing slogan: "It will leave you breathless." Like other spirits, though, the rise to stardom hit the speed bump known as the Sixties and Seventies, when drug and health fads predominated. Then, the California winemaking industry blossomed. Vodka and other spirits faded into the background.

Another brilliant marketing campaign, political upheaval and the avaricious culture of the 1980s resurrected vodka. The marketing came from Sweden's Absolut and gave vodka a young, sexy image attractive to younger drinkers. The political upheaval was, of course, the end of communism in Eastern Europe. Until then, the only Russian vodka available was Stoli, beginning in the 1970s as a part of a deal with Pepsi. After communism fell, other brands from Russia and Poland became available.

The rise in popularity of the cosmopolitan cocktail — thank you again, Hollywood — made other specialty flavored vodka based cocktails sexy and all the rage. Restaurants and bars around the country soon had extensive "martini" menus mostly consisting of fruity vodka drinks. Now vodka outranks all other spirits by about five to one. A look at your local liquor store shelves shows this trend is only growing.

Although most people think of cocktails when they think of vodka, and perhaps more specifically, sweet palatable cocktails, it can also be enjoyed neat or on the rocks. In Poland and Russia, vodka tasting is an art form. You can spend hours at a bar tasting vodka like you might taste wine on a tour through Napa. Traditionally, vodka straight up is served cold, either from the freezer or refrigerator. You might want to try an around-the-world sampling from Scandinavia, Poland, Russia, France and one of the new, excellent American craft-distilleries.

You don't have to put on your Polish folk costume to enjoy a vodka tasting, although costumes never hurt the mood of a party. Just raise your glass and say, "Na zdrowie!" Phonetically, that would be: naz-droh-vee-ay. Just say it fast enough and any Pole or Russian within earshot will know exactly what you mean!

"Na zdrowie!"

Kamikaze

2 ounces vodka
2 ounces triple sec
1 ounce lime juice

Combine in a cocktail shaker with ice.
Shake and strain into a cocktail glass.
Garnish with a lime twist if desired.

Some of us may remember a Kamikaze in a shot format from college, but the traditional recipe calls for 1:1:1 ratio of all ingredients and serves it straight up. Thirsty Jane's taste-testers found this made the drink too tart. Tweak the proportions and make this your drink.

The Barstool Buzz:

"Leaves you wanting more."

"A long, extended shot."

"It's a margarita for non-tequila people!"

Sea Breeze

2 ounces vodka
1 ounce grapefruit juice
3 ounces cranberry juice

Add vodka to highball glass and fill with ice. Add grapefruit juice and cranberry juice. Stir. Garnish with a lime wedge if desired.

Although a "starter" drink for many 1970s coeds, the Sea Breeze still does the job. It's a variation of the Cape Codder, which is simply vodka and cranberry juice. Other variations include the Bay Breeze (sub pineapple for grapefruit juice), the Greyhound (take out the cranberry), and the Madras (sub orange for grapefruit juice).

The Barstool Buzz:

"The perfect girlfriend drink for the patio."

"Can start this way before happy hour!"

"This could get way stronger and you'd hardly notice."

Harvey Wallbanger

2 ounces vodka
4 ounces orange juice
½ ounce Galliano

Add vodka to a highball glass and fill with
ice. Add orange juice. Float the Galliano on
top. Garnish with an orange twist if desired.

It may simply be a
Screwdriver with
Galliano on top,
but it delivers.
Original marketing from
the 1950s featured a
surfer named Harvey
who would run into
walls after having
one too many of these
Wallbangers.

The Barstool Buzz:

"Fun to drink. Unique combination of flavors."

"Love the licorice kick at the end."

*"Definitely something to drink with a straw, and
from the bottom up!"*

Moscow Mule

2 ounces vodka
4 ounces ginger beer
½ lime

Squeeze lime in highball glass, add vodka
and fill with ice. Add ginger beer. Stir gently.
Garnish with a lime wedge or twist if desired.

Ginger beer, not ginger
ale, makes the Moscow
Mule authentic and gives
it the spicy kick at the
end. Ginger beer is sold
at most grocery stores
with other specialty
sodas. If you find the
ginger too strong, try
using a little ginger ale
with the ginger beer.

The Barstool Buzz:

"Love the ginger."

"What a kick!"

"How can beer be stronger than ale?"

Mochacino

1 ounce vodka
1 ounce Kahlua
1 ounce Godiva White Chocolate Liqueur

Combine in a cocktail shaker with ice.
Shake and strain into a cocktail glass.

This Thirsty Jane original was the No. 1-rated drink from my panel of taste testers. Perfect for an after-dinner drink. This baby is dessert enough.

The Barstool Buzz:

"Dessert in a glass."

"I would drink this quite a lot."

"A candy bar in a glass, yet not too sweet."

Rum

Partying With the Pirates

What do reincarnation and rum have to do with one another? In all likelihood, not a thing, but often I wonder why the tropical ocean exerts an inexplicable pull on Thirsty Jane, despite the fact I am a landlubber through and through. Could I have been a sugarcane worker in a former life? Or a sword-wielding pirate? My affinity to a crescent of white powdery sand caressing an ocean cove the color of gummy sharks is elemental. Right there with me rests the ubiquitous rum punch in a container most people typically use for water on a grueling hour-long run. Well, the ice melts and dilutes the booze! Really.

Rum speaks to lazy afternoons on a sun-drenched beach with rhythmic waves lapping in the background. Pineapples, limes, coconuts, mangoes and other tropical fruit nuzzle with rum to create candy-like adult beverages. Rum is sexy and sultry with intimations of swashbuckling pirates and men in uniform. What's Thirsty Jane not to like? Yet, it also claims a much darker history as a part of the slave trade between Europe, the Caribbean colonies and Africa.

Deliciously Demonic

A culture's ingenuity for creating an alcoholic beverage out of readily available materials always deserves admiration. Different groups in Asia fermented sugarcane thousands of years ago. Not until the Europeans brought distillation methods to the Caribbean did rum come into existence, however. First, sugarcane, the basis of rum, needed to find its way into the Americas. Thank you Christopher Columbus, who planted the first cane on what is now Haiti!

The European powerhouses settled in and fought constantly over the Caribbean islands. Sugarcane fields dominated the landscape, completely deforesting many of the islands in the quest to satisfy the mother country's sweet tooth. Many trace the emergence of rum to the British-owned island of Barbados. Producing crystalized sugar from sugarcane is a difficult process, with molasses as the byproduct. At first, sugar producers tossed the molasses to the animals for feed. Some ingenious man noticed the stuff fermented easily, thus producing an alcoholic beverage. Someone else came up with the idea of distilling the fermented mash, and rum was created. Hallelujah!

Where the name "rum" came from is subject to debate, but the oft-referenced derivation from the term "rumbullion," English slang from the 1600s meaning "a great tumult," seems fitting enough for the spirit's colorful romp through history. Not wanting rum to compete with domestically produced spirits, such as gin or brandy, European countries banned the import of the spirit. All of that rum needed someplace to go. Pirates, the British Navy, and the American Colonies bellied up to the bar. Rum became a form of liquid gold for the next 100 years until the American Revolution.

Pirates were not the cavalier studs with golden hearts of bodice-ripper fictional fame. Instead, they ruthlessly terrorized the Caribbean while downing their allotted share of rum each day. Even so, who can resist the swashbuckling vibe? There is a saying at Thirsty Jane's bar: "It's not a party without the pirate." After a particularly raucous party at Thirsty Jane's, a plastic figurine of Captain Morgan of spiced rum renown mysteriously appeared in my driveway, with a stained blue potholder nearby — go figure. Because no one ever claimed the good Cap'n, he hangs out on the bar, a warning symbol of the consequences of debauchery. Or something like that.

Unfortunately, the real Captain Morgan didn't heed the warning sirens against excessive rumbullion. Sir Henry Morgan was an extraordinarily successful privateer, essentially a government-sanctioned pirate. After his career on the high seas ended, he returned to Jamaica as its governor. There, he drank himself to death. On rum. His likeness lives on, both on a bottle of spiced rum, and at Thirsty Jane's bar.

Legitimate sailors also partook liberally of the Caribbean's demon spirit. The British Royal Navy rationed a half-pint a day of rum to its sailors. That's more than five shots, per day, every day. Shiver me timbers! At one point, the fleet's top brass began watering down the rum, and adding a little sugar and lime juice. Grog, the first rum cocktail of sorts, whetted the British sailor's thirst for hundreds of years. Pusser's Rum, made in the British Virgin Islands, supplied the fleet. Thankfully, the public can now buy Pusser's Rum, which when made in the British Virgin Islands' Painkiller drink, is a remarkable way to spend the morning on the beach after your first night in the islands. So I've heard.

Rumming to America

If the pirates and Royal Navy's grog swillers weren't enough, take a look at the signers of the Declaration of Independence for boozing inspiration. Life in the American Colonies was not easy, and colonists imbibed liberally to take the edge off. Cheap and easy to obtain from other nearby British colonies, rum made its way into punches and coolers in place of the more expensive brandy. Even George Washington was an aficionado and served rum at the first inauguration.

Rum's history to this point has had its scuffles with life's shady side in the guise of pirates, men in uniform and colonial patriots. Rum's more sinister role in the slave trade cannot be ignored. Molasses from Caribbean colonies traveled to the American Colonies where it was distilled into rum. Traders took the rum to Africa to buy slaves, who were then transported back to the Caribbean to work in the cane fields to produce more sugar and, as a consequence, more molasses. The cycle continued until the American Revolution.

When American colonists tried to cut England out of the lucrative trade by buying molasses or rum from the French and Spanish, England passed the Molasses Act in 1733. This law taxed the importation of molasses into the American Colonies from countries other than England. American colonists thumbed their noses at the Brits, and a series of additional taxes were enacted and eventually rebellion ensued. We all know what happened.

Ironically, although rum helped ignite the American Revolution, the spirit soon disappeared from the boozing landscape. Sea trade was disrupted during the American Revolution and the production and distribution of rum shifted solely to the Caribbean region. At the same time, grain crops of corn,

wheat and rye increased in production, thus spawning the birth of whiskey as America's drink of choice, but that is another chapter.

Not until the beginning of the 20th century did rum resurface on the American drinking scene. By the end of the 1800s, the Bacardi distillery in Cuba refined the production of rum to create a lighter version that was smooth and easy to mix.

Two men with Teddy Roosevelt's Rough Riders concocted the Cuba Libre and the Daiquiri while in Cuba after sampling the new version of rum.

Americans took to the new drinks and traveled to nearby Cuba to enjoy legal liquor during Prohibition. Illegal importation of rum thrived during Prohibition because of the Caribbean's proximity to the U.S. Ships loaded down with Caribbean rum would dock in international waters off America's East Coast. Smaller boats called "rum runners" would deliver the caches to onshore distributors.

The rediscovery of rum during Prohibition laid the ground for its rapid growth after World War II. With the multitude of U.S. Navy bases in the Caribbean, servicemen were exposed to and took a liking to rum. In post-war years, they brought their tastes back to home life, and the tiki craze of the 1950s carried rum to the forefront where it remains one of America's most popular spirits.

Sweet Caribbean Conundrum

Selecting the right rum for your drink is confusing because no international standards regulate production of rum. Distilleries around the world make "rum." However, other than the name and a general agreement that the base must be sugarcane, production methods, aging requirements, categories and proof can vary significantly. Even in the Caribbean the differences between a Puerto Rican rum and a Jamaican rum are dramatic. Each type brings its unique flavor to a drink, which is why multiple types of specifically called-out rums grace a classic tiki-lounge drink, making it a work of mixology art.

In general, there are three categories of Puerto Rican rum: light (also known as silver or white), gold, and añejo or aged. Colorless, smooth and dry, light rum mixes well in cocktails and, for simplicity sake, is the base for all recipes in this book. Light rum is aged for only one year in stainless containers or oak barrels. Gold rum is basically light rum that has been aged slightly longer, perhaps up to three years, to enhance flavor and/or has had some caramel coloring added. The big difference comes with añejo rum, which usually spends more than five years in a barrel before bottling. These fine rums are suitable for sipping neat (straight).

Dark Jamaican rums emit a full-bodied aroma and taste. Unlike "lighter-bodied" rums, Jamaican rums are fermented for a longer period and use natural yeast. The mash then is double-distilled in pot stills to create a rich, powerful spirit. Like all alcohols, Jamaican rum comes off the still clear, but longer aging and the addition of coloring create the distinctive dark brown appearance. Jamaican rum finds a perfect home in drinks like planters' punch, a Colonial favorite, where a darker color and stronger flavor complement the sweetness of the fruit juices and added sugar.

Some distillers have followed vodka's lead and made flavored rums, running the gamut of fruity flavors to earthy spices and vanillas. Use of a flavored rum gives the mixologist endless options for expanding the characteristics of a drink. Because you don't use a flavored spirit frequently, collecting them can be pricey.

More than any other spirit, rum delivers almost endless options on color and flavor. Whether light and bright or dark and spicy, rum transports the drinker to another place and time. Sip it neat, mix it in a cocktail, or add some water and serve up the grog. Be a sailor, a pirate, a planter, a rebel, a Havana playboy, or a chilled-out beachcomber. Rum will take you where you want to go if you let her. Here's to rum, more than a great tumult!

R

Cuba Libre

2 ounces rum
4 ounces cola
Lime wedge

Add rum to highball glass. Fill with ice.
Add cola and squeeze lime wedge in.
Stir gently. Garnish with a lime wedge
if desired.

Yes, this is just a
rum and Coke with lime.
But asking for a
Cuba Libra is much sexier!
One story claims the
drink was invented
by soldiers of
Teddy Roosevelt's
Rough Riders who were
fighting Spain in Cuba
in the early 1900s.
Legend has it they toasted
to "Free Cuba."

The Barstool Buzz:

"Love what the lime does to it!"

"Doesn't get any simpler than this."

"I don't think I can drink the plain version ever again."

Daiquiri

2 ounces rum
½ ounce simple syrup
¾ ounce fresh lime juice

Combine in a cocktail shaker with ice.
Shake and strain into cocktail glass.
Garnish with a lime twist or slice
if desired.

A daiquiri is similar
to the British Navy's grog,
which was a mix of
rum, lime juice, water
and sugar. Tell the next
man's man who turns
his nose up at this drink
that both Hemingway and
President John F. Kennedy
were daiquiri lovers.
Make your own simple
syrup by boiling equal
parts water and
sugar until syrupy,
then cooling it.

The Barstool Buzz:

"My new Friday night drink!"

"So this is where it all began?"

"To hell with strawberries. All you need is lime."

Rum Rickey

2 ounces rum
4 ounces club soda
Juice from ½ lime

Add rum to highball glass. Fill with ice.
Add club soda and lime juice.
Stir gently. Garnish with a lime wedge if desired.

A "rickey" is made
using any liquor with
lime juice and club soda.
Try a gin rickey,
applejack rickey, or even
a bourbon rickey.
For friends on the wagon,
make them a rickey
with grape juice and
a little grenadine in
addition to the
lime and club soda.

The Barstool Buzz:

"Ah, summer in a glass!"

"Fresh lime makes all the difference."

"I've had other rickeys, but rickey was made for rum."

Loco Coco

1 ounce rum
1 ounce fresh lime juice
1 ounce cream of coconut

Combine in a cocktail shaker with ice.
Shake and strain into cocktail glass.
Garnish with a slice of lime if desired.

Cream of coconut is a
thick, creamy, sugary
piece of heaven
made from the heart of a
coconut and sugarcane.
Yes, it is full of fat,
sugar and calories.
Get over it and make
the damned drink!
You will not
be disappointed.

The Barstool Buzz:

"Yummy!"

"Oh. My. God. This is good."

"A seven-day Caribbean cruise in a glass."

Piña Colada

1 ounce rum
1 ounce pineapple juice
1 ounce cream of coconut

Blend with a cup of ice and a pinch of salt
in blender. Pour into a cocktail glass.
Garnish with fresh pineapple and/or a
maraschino cherry if desired.

Several bars in San Juan,
Puerto Rico claim title
to the invention of the
Piña Colada, but most
attribute it to the bartender
at the Caribe Hilton Hotel.
Although Thirsty Jane
is not a big fan of an
over-sweet drink, a
Piña Colada is irresistible,
especially if you are
anywhere near the
vicinity of a beach or
even a baby pool.

The Barstool Buzz:

"Just an umbrella away from perfection."

"The premixed versions can't compare."

"Makes me want to get caught in the rain and give up yoga."

Tequila

Passion and Drama, From Mezcal to Margarita

In a dive bar next to the railroad tracks in a ubiquitous Midwestern college town, "Tequila!" rang out in unison. The piano-banging geriatric chanteuse paused as the horde of coeds — a young, naive version of Thirsty Jane included — rushed the bar for a shot. That much, at least, I remember accurately. I think. Pretty sure.

Tequila, a spirit born of an Aztec goddess with 400 breasts (settle down, boys), ignites passions, both amorous and aggressive, and sometimes aggressively amorous. Based upon my collective undergrad experiences with tequila, I once flirtingly warned my future husband not to drink tequila with me. He promptly and disappointingly agreed to abstain from the nectar of the ancient gods. Luckily, he's a smart man and learned that sarcasm and Thirsty Jane go hand in hand. Tequila is now a household staple for us, as it is in many homes. But this unique spirit was not always a favorite of or even available to mere mortals.

Aztec mythology offers several captivating explanations of the origins of tequila and the agave plant from which it is made. My personal favorite is the story woven from the same cloth as a reality TV show. The drama starts with a bitchy controlling goddess who saps light from the universe. A hunky redemptive god zooms up to the sky to show her who's boss. Instead of taking care of business, hunky god falls for the light-sucking goddess' granddaughter, who just happens to be a fertility goddess with 400 breasts. As you can imagine, this does not sit well with the evil grandmother who tracks down the happy couple and slays the granddaughter. Hunky god gets his revenge by killing the grandmother goddess and restoring light to the universe, but his multi-breasted lover is gone. She has transformed into the agave plant, and the sap she produces provides him peace, not to mention the bonus hallucinogenic experiences.

New World, New Booze, New Buzz

For thousands of years, the Aztec priests and nobility partook of pulque, the precursor to tequila, as part of religious ceremonies. Everything changed in the 1500s when Spanish conquistadors "discovered" the New World. The thirsty Spaniards ran into trouble after they guzzled down their ration of brandy. The military's need to imbibe played a huge part in the development of modern-day tequila. With all the brandy and wine depleted, the Spaniards turned to indigenous booze. After knocking back the native pulque, the conquistadors recognized distillation could radically improve the newfound booze.

Around 1600, large-scale distillation of a spirit from the mezcal plant began in the Mexican town of Tequila, in the state of Jalisco. For the next 200 years, "mezcal wine" grew in production and consumption throughout Mexico. During the 1700s, the Spanish government licensed the production of mezcal, and producers such as Don Jose María Guadalupe De Cuervo and Don Cenobio Sauza began serious mezcal manufacturing.

By the 1880s, the transcontinental railroads made exportation of mezcal to the United States possible. Mezcal, now known as tequila, took root in America. In the early 20th century, the Mexican tequila industry organized and modernized to produce greater quantities of higher-grade tequila.

However, powerful landowners, including the tequila producing haciendas, had to reckon with the popular movement as the Mexican Revolution raged from 1910-1920. The revolutionary soldiers sought solace during wartime and turned to tequila. Produced in Jalisco, one of the uprising's major battle areas, tequila acquired a reputation as a rebel's drink. Tequila segued from the Mexican Revolution bandits to American speakeasies during Prohibition. Proximity to the supply chain meant Southwestern bootleggers and speakeasies made tequila the drink of choice during the "dry" period.

Just as Prohibition ended and tequila gained traction with American consumers, Mexico suffered an agave shortage. Unlike other spirits, which are produced from annually grown crops, tequila requires mature blue agave plants. Thanks to the plant's 8 to 12-year maturation rate, crop failure can devastate the tequila industry for a decade or more.

To combat the shortage, tequila makers mixed the blue agave spirit with a neutral spirit made from sugar — un-aged rum, in other words. For the next 30 years, only "mixto" tequila, made from at least 51 percent tequila, was imported into the U.S. Until recently, mixto dominated the market. Although mixto tequila is not suitable for sipping, it makes a perfectly good cocktail.

The creation of the margarita cocktail in the mid 1940s upgraded tequila's status in the U.S. Like the origin of the agave plant, the true story behind the margarita's creation remains elusive. Mexico's Ministry of Tequila subscribes to the legend of bartender Francisco "Pancho" Morales of Tommy's Bar in Juarez. A customer ordered a drink Morales had never heard of, so he faked it. "Olé!" says Thirsty Jane to that one!

Other tales link the drink to bartender Danny Herrera in Tijuana concocting the drink for a Hollywood wannabe, Marjorie King, and naming it after the Spanish variation of her name. Another fame-laced story traces the margarita back to Dallas socialite Margarita Sames who allegedly mixed up the drink for some of her elite friends, including a hotel-owner named Hilton, in 1948 Acapulco. Whatever or whoever the inspiration, the tequila and lime cocktail found an audience in the U.S. where it reigns as the most popular mixed drink.

As tequila's popularity skyrocketed, the Mexican government took steps to ensure only certain Mexican producers could use the name "tequila." Only five regions in Mexico may make tequila. This is similar to the French government's requirement that only sparkling wine made from grapes of the Champagne region may be called "champagne." All tequila is aged in Mexico, but a large proportion is shipped in bulk to the U.S. for bottling and distribution.

The regulatory changes improved the quality of tequila by eliminating the watered-down spirits and those not made with blue agave. Then a deadly bacteria devastated the blue agave crop in the late 1990s straining the market, just as tequila's popularity and demand for 100 percent blue agave tequila surged in the U.S.

Although production has increased dramatically over tequila's history, methods remain true to tradition. A blue agave plant is a succulent, not a cactus, and grows spiky leaves up to seven feet that surround a heart. Harvesters, called jimadors, cut the plants by hand and trim back the spiky leaves to leave the heart or piña. A mature piña typically weighs between 60 and 120 pounds. The first step in making tequila is to cook the piñas in an oven for at least a day. Next, the piñas are milled to extract as much juice as possible. For pure agave tequila, the juice ferments with natural yeast in tanks. For mixto, diluted sugarcane or molasses is added along with commercial yeast. Double distillation of the fermented brew is done in copper stills with the end result of 80 to 92 proof clear tequila. Some tequila is aged in wooden tanks up to four years, which imparts in the liquor the colors and flavors of the wood and makes it suitable for sipping.

True Blue or Mixto? Both!

When you shop for tequila, consider what you will be using the tequila for. Are you making a punch bowl of margaritas for a crowd? Looking to sip it neat? Making just a cocktail here and there for yourself and friends? All of the recipes in this chapter are best with a 100 percent blue agave blanco, which might also be called plata or platinum. This version is un-aged, making it clear and perfect for mixing, as it does not have an aged tequila's complex flavors to interfere with your mixes. The gold tequila of my youth doesn't sit on my bar. It's usually a mixto and not as clean as the 100 percent blue agave blancos, which are often not much more expensive. But, as Thirsty Jane is famous for doing at a party, if you are mixing the gargantuan punch bowl of "trailer park margs" loaded with sugar and whatnot, then, by all means, aim low. No one will know or care.

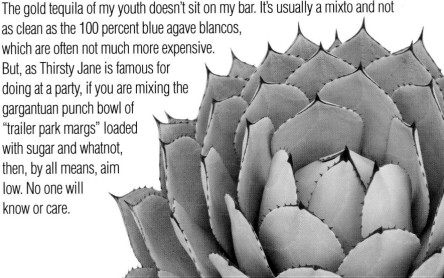

Aged tequila can be either reposado, meaning it's aged 3 to 12 months, or añejo, meaning old and aged up to four years in Kentucky bourbon barrels. Manufacturers vary on whether the barrels are charred and how many times they are reused. Both reposado and añejo tequilas can be mixto or 100 percent blue agave. Both are best suited for sipping. So don't waste your money on one of these expensive bottles for a margarita or get hornswoggled at a bar into turning over half your paycheck for an añejo in your mixed drink.

If most margaritas you drink are neon green, experiment with the recipes in this chapter to acclimate your palate to agave. Once you feel comfortable with a drink in which you taste the tequila and not just the sugar, and if your wallet is healthy enough, try tasting some tequila straight. Buy a 100-percent agave reposado or añejo. Serve the tequila in a tulip-shaped small wineglass. Leave the salt and lime wedge to the coeds. As with all liquor tastings, first check out the color. Unless caramel coloring is used, darker tequila has been aged longer. Next get a good whiff of the stuff. Do you smell the unique agave? Are there any other discernible scents? Finally, take a sip and let it sit in your mouth as you think of the flavors. When you swallow, note whether it is smooth or burns. Not everyone will want to sip tequila, but a great tequila is worthy of sipping like a great scotch or cognac. Only you can say whether you are ready. Remember, Thirsty Jane judges not a boozer's preferences, but always encourages you to drink what you like.

What happened to mezcal? Mezcal is still around and making its way into cocktails, but even Thirsty Jane admits it's a bit of an acquired taste. All tequila is considered mezcal, but not all mezcals are tequila because they are not made from blue agave from the designated regions. In making mezcal, the piña is often smoked and the fermentation lasts much longer than it does for tequila. The pungency and smokiness faces forward in mezcal, but give it a try next time you run across a cocktail containing this spirit.

Thirsty Jane has come a long way from slamming shots at the railroad tracks lounge in college days. A carefully crafted cocktail or a sophisticated sipping añejo are my preferred ways to drink tequila now. As the crop that replaced the damaged plants at the turn of the century reaches maturity, we can look forward to continued expansion of …

"Tequila!"

Juanita's Rita

1 ½ ounces tequila
1 ounce triple sec
½ ounce fresh lime juice

Combine with ice in a cocktail shaker.
Shake and strain into a cocktail glass,
rimmed with salt if you wish. Garnish with
a lime wedge if desired.

Around the Rim
Salt or no salt is an
essential question for your
guests. To salt a rim,
pour course salt onto
a small plate.
Run a lime wedge
around the edge of the
glass and dip the glass
straight down into the salt.
Shake off any excess.
Salt ahead of time
when serving a crowd.

The Barstool Buzz:

"Oh so smooth."

"Wouldn't mind a double!"

"I could guzzle this."

Paloma

2 ounces tequila
½ ounce fresh lime juice
4 ounces grapefruit soda

Add tequila and lime juice to highball glass.
Fill glass with ice. Add soda and stir lightly.
Garnish with a lime wedge or cherry if desired.

Did You Know?
The Paloma, not the margarita, is the most popular tequila-based cocktail in Mexico. Perfect for sipping on the patio on a hot summer day, the Paloma is sinfully simple, which makes it a Thirsty Jane fave!

The Barstool Buzz:

"Refreshing."

"A drink for sitting outside in the summer."

"Why have I been drinking margs all these years?"

Bloody Maria

2-3 sprigs of cilantro
2 ounces tequila
4 ounces Bloody Mary mix

Muddle cilantro in bottom of highball
glass with a little of the tequila. Add rest of
tequila. Fill glass with ice. Add Bloody Mary
mix and stir. Garnish with a
lime wedge, olive, or jalapeño
pepper, if desired.

The Bloody Maria is
nothing but a Bloody
Mary where tequila
replaces the vodka.
Try experimenting with
add-ins like jalepeños,
Worcestershire sauce,
lime juice, Tabasco,
etc. to put your own
signature on this drink.

The Barstool Buzz:

"Better than the vodka version."

"Salsa in a drink."

"Forget the celery. Give me a jalapeno."

Brave Bull

1 ½ ounces tequila
1 ounce Kahlua

Add to double old-fashioned glass filled
with ice. Stir gently.

The Brave Bull is
best as an after-dinner
drink. (Change the tequila
to vodka and you have
a Black Russian.)
Like any matador or
torero will tell you,
it takes some guts to
go toe to toe with
the Brave Bull.
The rewards?
It sure beats a kick
in the head.

The Barstool Buzz:

"For the strong at heart."

"A hearty nightcap."

"This feels like it's taking me by the horns."

La Playa

1 ½ ounces tequila
½ ounce blue curaçao
1 ounce pineapple juice

Combine with ice in a cocktail shaker. Shake and strain into cocktail glass. Garnish with a piece of pineapple if desired.

Blue curaçao is an orange-flavored liqueur which, when combined with pineapple juice, produces a drink the color of the Caribbean Sea.
Sit back, take a sip, and imagine the warm ocean waves lapping at your feet.

The Barstool Buzz:

"Beach bar drink at home."

"How can something so blue taste so orange?"

"Tastes like it should only be served at a swim-up bar."

Whiskey

Don't Fear the Dark Spirit. Rebel!

Whiskey intimidates me.

Single-malt, blended, small-batch, single-barrel, American, Canadian, Scotch, Irish, bonded, rye, bourbon, Tennessee, corn. Last but not least, is it "whisky" or "whiskey"? Before we go any further, let me answer that question. The Scots and Canadians spell it "whisky," and the Americans and Irish spell it "whiskey." For consistency, I will use the American spelling throughout, recognizing that I'm technically incorrect when referring to Scotch and Canadian whiskey.

Cruising the whiskey aisle at the liquor store, I must look like a lost sheep because one of the managers inevitably comes over and asks if I need help. It only takes a few moments before I realize I'm sweating and spluttering and stammering because I don't even know where to start. Afraid of looking like a complete moron, I usually just blurt out something totally ridiculous like, "Where's the gin?"

Yet, for all the angst and confusion, whiskey has a special place in my heart. Many years ago, not too long after the dinosaurs disappeared, Thirsty Jane and a pack of young girls would cavort around the dance floor at family weddings in a certain Midwestern city. They would surreptitiously nip at their moms' highballs. Just one or two teensy drinks, that's all. They'd dance for hours, run around like wildlings and hide under the folded-up bleachers in the gymnasium where the wedding reception was held. They didn't know it back then, but that was whiskey in their moms' highball. And it was love at first guzzle. Sip, I mean.

Yet, upon reaching adulthood, the myriad options on the whiskey shelves at the liquor store scared me. With limited resources, I didn't want to choose unwisely. So I just moved on and hit the gin aisle where the brands were fewer and the options less divergent. For years I avoided whiskey until someone gave me a really nice bottle of single-malt scotch for a birthday. After a night spent suffering through a long and contentious meeting of a community board, I looked at that bottle of scotch and wondered if it might be able to make me forget the backbiting and bring back those happy-go-lucky childhood moments. I poured a little over a few ice cubes, swirled the glass, and...

Praise Jesus, amen! That was the ticket.

Still, I avoided buying whiskey until I started mixing cocktails and some revelers asked for Manhattans. With a little reading and a lot of help from the nice people at the liquor store, I started to experiment. If you've ever felt perplexed by the difference between scotch and bourbon, stay tuned. It's not as hard as I once thought and the bottom line, like all my advice on boozing, is that you should drink what you like and not get caught up in what is cool or hip. You are cool and hip for just putting yourself out in the universe as a mixer and shaker.

Beam Me Up, Or Is It Scotty?

One of the best places to begin this whiskey education is Scotland. Although probably not born in Scotland, whiskey grew to prominence there. Precise knowledge of whiskey's birth is elusive, but many point to a set of delivery records from Scottish monks in the late 1400s. There was enough malt for thousands of bottles of whiskey, so more likely than not, that delivery wasn't a first-timer's experiment with a still. Probably the Scots learned about distillation from their Irish counterparts who likely picked up the techniques from their journeys. First used medicinally (isn't that what they all say?!) and under church control (didn't they regulate every pleasure?!), whiskey soon migrated to small artisanal distilleries for extra-medicinal use.

All was going swimmingly until the government realized it could generate some needed revenues by taxing not only the end product, but also the stills and the ingredients that went into making scotch. By 1707, when England and Scotland united politically, discontent among Scottish distillers ran high. The rugged Highlanders of northern Scotland thumbed their noses at the taxmen and took bootlegging to an art form. Meanwhile, the Lowlands' distillers showed a willingness to play the government's game and found a market in England. Large distilleries began to produce legally their own form of scotch that was not exclusively made of the taxed malt. This signaled the beginning of the rift, which still runs today, between the Highlands' craft-oriented, single-malt scotch and the blends of the Lowlands' corporate distilleries.

Today, scotch is either a single-malt or a blend of grain whiskey and malt whiskey. The "malt" comes from barley. First, the raw grain soaks in water for several days, then is spread out on a floor where it germinates over the course of a week or so. The germinated barley, or malt, dries in ovens. Peat, used for fuel to dry the malt for Highland scotch, imparts a distinctive dark, earthy undertone to the spirit, very different from the coal-fired oven of a Lowland distillery.

In the next stage of production, the malt is ground, mixed with water, and then fermented. The fermented product is distilled twice in pot stills. After distillation, the whiskey settles down in oak barrels for a minimum of three years, but more likely between 10 and 25. After aging, a small amount of the malt scotch is bottled into single-malt scotch, but most of it winds up part of the blended scotch market.

Blended scotch is mostly grain whiskey, typically made with wheat or corn. In addition to the different grain used, the whiskey is distilled in a column still which results in a smoother, although less flavorful, whiskey. A blender will utilize a few different grain whiskeys along with up to dozens of malt whiskeys to craft the final product. While whiskey connoisseurs may look down on them, blends offer a consistent product at a value-oriented price. A blend is perfectly fine for use in a cocktail. Save the pricey single-malts for sipping neat or with a splash of water or a few ice cubes.

The 20th century's wars and economic downturns took their toll on the scotch industry. Many distilleries converted to industrial alcohol production during World War I. By the time distillers were ready to ramp up again, American Prohibition was in full swing. Spirits like gin that were easy to produce at home became popular. The Great Depression further dampened Americans' taste for scotch. Another war, a gin-oriented cocktail culture, and more economic instability racked the scotch industry. Finally, during the prosperous 1980s and 1990s, Americans sought out high-end spirits and cultivated the single-malt scotch cult. Appreciation for a fine single-malt continues, but as we begin returning to cocktails, the market for a good blended scotch remains stable.

So what about Irish whiskey? Sadly, even though the Irish introduced whiskey to the Scots, the Irish were not able to sustain their development of the spirit. The events that negatively affected scotch also impacted Irish whiskey. Additionally, the famine in the mid 1800s decimated Ireland's distilling industry. Finally, when Ireland became independent of the United Kingdom in 1922, British trade embargoes destroyed the markets for Irish whiskey. A conglomerate now makes most Irish whiskey, but

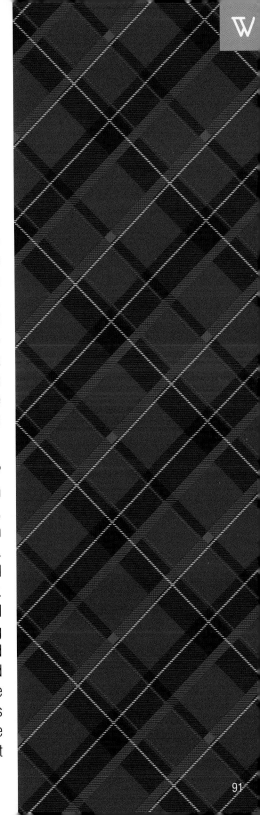

a few new independent distillers are resurrecting the craft of Irish whiskey. Like scotch, Irish whiskey can either be single-malt or blended. The distillation process the Irish follow is similar to that of the the Scots. Irish single-malts lack some of the smokiness of the Scottish ones, however, because as the malt is dried, the ovens isolate the smoke from the grain.

That's a lot of information and we haven't crossed the Atlantic yet. Luckily, whiskey's evolution in North America has some parallels with its progression in the U.K.

Rebel Yell

Something about whiskey distillers invokes the vibe of the rebel. Whether in the Scottish Highlands or the western hills of Pennsylvania, the early makers of whiskey stood united against "the man," otherwise known as the taxman.

Immigrants from Scotland, by way of Ireland, settled the frontiers of American Colonies like Pennsylvania, Maryland and Virginia. They grew mostly corn and rye but found it easier to distill the grains and trade the liquor instead of transporting spoilable grains to markets. Just like in Scotland, though, the government got greedy. With serious debt to repay from the Revolutionary War, the U.S. government imposed the first American tax. On whiskey.

This did not sit well with the Scotch-Irish settlers who had just left their homeland to get free from "the man." Settlers in western Pennsylvania took up arms, but with a massive 12,000-soldier show of force, President George Washington, himself a distiller of whiskey, crushed what would come to be known as the Whiskey Rebellion.

Fleeing, the rebellious farmers moved further west into Kentucky where they continued to distill their whiskey, now made primarily from corn. The barrels of booze shipped downriver to New Orleans bore the stamp of origin, Bourbon County. This location would become synonymous with the unique form of whiskey although bourbon is no longer made there.

Unlike scotch whiskey, bourbon is made with a sour mash, similar to how sour dough bread is made. During fermentation, some of the already fermented mash that was held back from the previous batch is added. After a double distillation in pot stills, the bourbon is set to age for a minimum of two years in charred oak barrels. Before bottling, most bourbon is filtered to ensure clarity in the bottle.

Once the barrels began flowing from Kentucky, bourbon was poised to become the American spirit. However, just when bourbon had taken root, the Civil War tore apart the states that produced most of it. After the war, taxes were again imposed to pay off debt. The rest of bourbon's story looks a lot like scotch's: World War I, Prohibition, Depression, World War II, and the rise of white spirits in cocktails. Bourbon's continued decline in the 1960s and '70s followed that of all hard liquor as Americans turned to wine and recreational drugs. The survival of America's whiskey seemed questionable. Fortunately, single-malt scotch's appeal facilitated a similar revival of premium bourbon. Many posh bars now feature lists of bourbon longer than some restaurants' wine lists.

Wait! That's not all, folks You may also run across "rye whiskey," "Tennessee whiskey" and "Canadian whisky" in stores and in cocktail books. You can spend a small fortune on different types of whiskey if you follow every recipe to a "T." When in doubt, use a blended scotch and reasonably priced bourbon. But just in case you need a little tidbit of cocktail knowledge, here we go. Tennessee whiskey is essentially Jack Daniels, although a few other distillers make this type of whiskey. It's a lot like bourbon, but goes through a filtration process in the end to remove some of the flavors.

Rye whiskey is the whiskey traditionally used in a Manhattan, although many recipes call for, and mixologists are comfortable with, bourbon. Rye is making a comeback through artisanal distilleries. It is whiskey made predominately with rye, which gives it a full, more assertive, perhaps even rougher taste. Canadian whiskeys are blends. They took off in the U.S. market after Prohibition when American distilleries were not ready to bring whiskey to the market. Canadians had been stockpiling whiskey and blended it with lighter whiskey or a neutral spirit to stretch the stockpiles. The lighter-style blends were perfect introductory whiskeys and great for mixing in highballs.

> A highball is 1 ½ ounces of whiskey with 4 ounces of your favorite mixer, such as club soda, ginger ale, tonic, or cola. Thirsty Jane prefers just a slightly boozier drink and usually pours in 2 ounces, but I'm a lush.

On Bourbon, Blends, Batches and Bartenders

Whiskey is so diverse, it's easy to feel intimidated. When all else fails, get a bottle of bourbon or a bottle of blended scotch. Don't be afraid to ask your liquor store manager for his or her recommendation in a certain price range. You can usually get something great for mixing cocktails for under $20.

If you have some money burning a hole in your pocket and want to sample some exquisite bourbon, try a small-batch or single-barrel bourbon. "Small-batch" means the blender picks a few select barrels of premium bourbon and blends them to make a particularly tasty product. "Single-barrel" means just that — bourbon bottled from one specifically selected barrel.

Although buying a drink in a bar is much more expensive per serving than purchasing a whole bottle, you might want to experiment before investing in an expensive bottle of whiskey. One of my favorite ways to do this is mooching off my whiskey-snob friends. They are always eager to let me sample their latest finds and compare different types. Alternatively, most serious bartenders similarly enjoy sharing their passion for booze with curious customers. You'd be surprised how many free sips you can get if you take the time to pick a bartender's mind. Slow nights are best for this, but I've spent more than a few nights in a packed bar sampling the spirits or drinks of which a bartender is particularly proud.

Although some claim that whiskey is a "man's" drink, many self-confessed vodka-loving women taste-testers found, to their surprise, several cocktails in this section which they liked. The "dark spirits" can be an acquired taste, to be sure. Some of us got an early start on acquiring this taste, so a glass of neat scotch or bourbon is about as close to heaven as I've come. But nothing beats a Presbyterian highball when I'm looking for a light drink suitable for serving in a water bottle when doing the gardening.

Raise your glass to the rebel in you and have a whiskey!

Manhattan

2 ounces rye whiskey (or bourbon)
1 ounce sweet vermouth
2 dashes angostura bitters

Combine in a cocktail shaker with ice. Shake and strain into cocktail glass. Some prefer to stir this drink to improve clarity. Garnish with a maraschino cherry if desired.

Three for the Money
The Manhattan is one of the oldest and booziest cocktails around.
First publication of the recipe dates back to 1884 and was similar to the one still used today.
If you have scotch, substitute that to make a Rob Roy. Irish whiskey in the drink will give you an Emerald.

The Barstool Buzz:

"A warm and cozy classic. The epitome of a cocktail."

"If you're not drinking your whiskey neat, drink this one."

"Warms the heart and grows hair where you want it."

Rusty Nail

2 ounces scotch
1 ounce Drambuie

Build over ice in a double old-fashioned glass.

When I found this recipe, I shared it with a scotch-boozing girlfriend. Her response, "Oh, Gawd, that sounds divine!" Indeed it is, justifying Drambuie's claims to be the drink that satisfies. It was the personal liqueur of Bonnie Prince Charlie who tried, but failed, to restore the Stuarts to the British throne in 1746.

The Barstool Buzz:

"Training wheels for fledgling scotch drinkers."

"Sends a shiver down my liver."

"Didn't know scotch could taste so good without soda!"

Presbyterian

1½ ounces bourbon
2 ounces club soda
2 ounces ginger ale

Add bourbon to a highball glass and fill
with ice. Add in club soda and ginger ale.
Stir gently.

Also known as
the Press, this highball
was *the* drink of
choice for many
women in the 1950s.
It's light, of course.
Would you want your
Junior League ladies
pulling a naked
dance party on
the card tables after
a bridge game and
one too many
Presbyterians?

The Barstool Buzz:

"More potent than it tastes."

"Reminds me of a naughty Southern belle."

"Divine intervention."

Godfather

2 ounces scotch
1 ounce amaretto

Build over ice in a double old-fashioned glass.

The drink has nothing to do with the famous movie other than amaretto, which takes the edge off the scotch, being the official liqueur of Italy. Amaretto is thought to be an almond liqueur but is actually made with the pits of apricot trees grown near Milan. One legend has it that a young widow invented the drink and gave it to a painter as a thank-you. Supposedly, the drink worked wonders and sparked a romance between the two.

The Barstool Buzz:

"This is made to be an after-dinner drink."

"Amaretto rocks."

"Somebody made me a drink I can't refuse."

Satin Sheets

1 ounce bourbon
1 ounce half and half
1 ounce crème de cacao

Combine in a cocktail shaker with ice. Shake and strain into cocktail glass.

A Thirsty Jane variation on the Bourbon Satin, which, interestingly, has brandy in it, not bourbon. This one pleased both the ladies and gents in the crowd, as it's not too sweet and has enough substance to it, yet still goes down smooth. Perfect for an after-dinner drink for your bourbon-loving friends.

The Barstool Buzz:

"I expected sweet and sensual, and that's what I got."

"Tasty, mellow dessert drink."

"Hits the (wet) spot."

Whatnot

What's Not to Be Overlooked

A whatnot is "any of various other things that might also be mentioned" according to Webster's Dictionary. Every drink in this chapter is a bit of an oddball. They might be mentioned, but don't exactly fit in with the other categories. Because the ingredients aren't used in many of the other drinks in this book, you might hesitate on investing in some of these more unusual liquors. However, these drinks are so good they almost universally earned a "pour me another" rating by taste-testers making them deserving of your attention.

By now you should have picked up on the fact Thirsty Jane is an "equal opportunity boozer." Almost every kind of booze is tasty to me in its own special way. Picking a favorite cocktail is easy — the martini — but picking my next five favorites is another story. The reason for this chapter is that several of my favorites are "whatnots," including classics like the Jack Rose and Sidecar. And a Kir Royale should be compulsory before any fancy meal. Once you learn how to make these drinks, you will appreciate a great bartender's artistry whenever you order one.

Burn Baby, Burn

Brandy is a perfect place to start this hopscotch game through the whatnots because it, or a liquor that is part brandy, figures into three of the cocktails in this chapter. It is also the oldest distilled spirit in the world. For that reason, brandy evokes for me the image of old codgers in tweed jackets sitting in leather club chairs swirling their amber-colored cognac in big bowled glasses, chatting about world leaders like I might gossip about who just sent a snarky e-mail. Then cultural whiplash hits, and the image of hip-hop artists rapping about putting back cognac invades my thoughts. Talk about strange bedfellows!

Often the strangest bedfellows are the most interesting, and in the case of brandy, and cognac specifically, adoption of the spirit by the young hip-hop culture helped to revive a spirit that seemed to be on life-support at the musty old white guys club. The birth of the hard-liquor variety of booze goes all the way back to the Moors' invasion of Spain in the eighth century. The Moors brought with them knowledge of distillation for purposes of making medicine (likely story, eh?). Spanish monks began distilling wine to create a "burned wine." The burned wine then traveled to Italy where Dutch traders discovered and began shipping it. The Dutch word for burned wine was "brandewijn," a precursor to the drink's common name.

Straight brandewijn was probably pretty harsh stuff coming off the still. Serendipitously, Dutch shippers noticed the wine tasted much better after a long voyage in wooden casks. This led to the process of aging brandy, which is now a crucial part of its production. Essentially, brandy is a distillate of any fruit, but usually is made with grapes. The wine is double-distilled in pot stills, which allows for a good amount of flavor from the wine to stay in the alcohol. The new brandy is aged in oak casks for a minimum of two years, although most brandies stay in there much longer. The brandy starts in new oak but is transferred to used barrels to smooth out the taste. The most well-known of all the brandies is cognac.

Like champagne, bordeaux or burgundy wines, cognac is produced only from grapes grown in a certain region of France — in this case Cognac, on the country's western coast. The area was a natural shipping point of origin, so as the French began producing cognac brandy, the Dutch took it across the channel to England where it was a wild success. British distillers, including the familiar names of Martell and Hennessy, moved to the Cognac region and perfected the art of making brandy. By the mid 1800s, industries supporting brandy production made the Cognac region incredibly prosperous. When the phylloxera pest hit France in 1875, however, it nearly destroyed the cognac-producing vines. Even today, the vineyards are smaller than they were 150 years ago.

Picking a brandy can be perplexing. Do you buy cognac or brandy or what? And what's the deal with the stars and the letters on the label? How old is good? Unless you are looking for seriously yummy cognac to drink straight, you are fine buying a V.S., which stands for "very superior," or a three-star cognac for mixed drinks. These brandies are aged a minimum of two years but typically spend four to five years in the oak. The next fancier type is V.S.O.P. ("very, superior, old, pale") or five-star, usually aged between 10 and 15 years. X.O., or "Napoleon" cognac, is the priciest. Unless you have a wad to blow, just walk on past these in the liquor store.

Closely related to brandy is applejack, a distinctly American spirit. Applejack dates back to the 1700s when Colonists distilled hard apple cider. Today's applejack is made with 35 percent apple brandy and 65 percent neutral spirits. Because about six pounds of apples are used in every bottle of applejack, it has a fruity, mellow flavor, yet it is not sweet like a liqueur. This makes it an excellent base for a cocktail.

Too Sweet to Pass Up

Finally, a few words about liqueurs, those exotically flavored and colored alcoholic beverages that lend life to great cocktails and have made many a teenager violently ill after imprudent overindulgence. A shot of peppermint schnapps anyone? Ah, no.

In most cases, a neutral spirit is the base of a liqueur. For some, like Drambuie and Irish cream liqueurs, whiskey is the base. Sugar syrup is added to the base spirit to make the liqueur sweet. Depending upon the type of liqueur, the percentage of sugar will vary from 20 to 40 percent. The "crème" types of liqueur tend to be the sweetest.

Liqueurs' history dates back well before the Middle Ages when Mediterranean cultures distilled liqueurs from fruits like grapes and dates. Eventually, by the 12th century, the process found its way to Europe. The earliest European distillers were monks who probably had a little bit more time on their hands to experiment with various infusions of herbs, spices and fruits into the "water of life." Social enjoyment got a boost from Italian socialite Catherine de Medici who brought liqueurs to courtly life in the 1500s. Before long, the Dutch, Germans and French got in the game and began producing their own liqueurs.

The popularity of liqueurs continued to grow, reaching a peak in the Belle Epoque era, the end of the 1800s through World War I. Probably not coincidentally, the cocktail was born and matured during this time. Liqueurs continue to be popular today as they can be enjoyed on the rocks for an after-dinner drink or combined with other spirits to craft unique cocktails.

Some common liqueurs used as ingredients in this book are amaretto (almond flavored), crème de cacao, chocolate liqueur, coffee liqueur, crème de cassis (black currant flavored), orange liqueur, Irish cream liqueur, Galliano and Drambuie. The most used and versatile liqueur is an orange-flavored one. Triple sec is a

value-oriented version that does well in most cocktails. However, try Cointreau and Gran Marnier if you can afford them — you will taste the differences. Cointreau is my choice for a margarita or sidecar, but if I'm making a B-52 shot, I'll use Gran Marnier because it is so rich and smooth.

Like all boozes, what you pour is a point of personal preference, and you should never feel you have to like one type of liqueur over another. Every booze has its moment: It may be a big honkin' glass of Bailey's while kicking back with my B.F.F. watching *Pride and Prejudice* (again), or it could be some amaretto on the rocks in a swanky hotel bar after going to the theater with a date.

As Ralph Waldo Emerson said: "All life is an experiment. The more experiments you make, the better." Resist the urge to have the usual and, instead, order a … whatnot.

Sidecar

1½ ounces V.S. cognac
¾ ounce orange-flavored liqueur*
½ ounce lemon juice

Combine with ice in a cocktail shaker.
Shake and strain into a cocktail glass.
Garnish with a lemon twist if desired.

*such as triple sec, Cointreau
or Gran Marnier

Although there are conflicting stories about who invented the Sidecar, where and when, it remains a classic and may be the most famous Prohibition-era cocktail. Its ancestor is a Brandy Crusta from the late 1800s and its progeny is the Margarita — all you do is change the cognac to tequila and lemon juice to lime!

The Barstool Buzz:

"Classic and classy drink."

"Love the dry tartness."

"Strong finisher."

Kir Royale

Champagne/sparkling wine
½ ounce crème de cassis

Fill champagne flute with champagne/ sparkling wine, pour in crème de cassis.

> This is *the* aperitif (or pre-dinner drink to stimulate your appetite) in France. Variations include Kir, made with dry white wine instead of champagne, or Kir Imperiale, which substitutes raspberry liqueur for the crème de cassis.

The Barstool Buzz:

"What a gorgeous drink!"

"Love the gentle taste of the black current."

"Oui, oui!"

Port Lemonade

2 ounces ruby port
4 ounces lemonade

Add port to highball class and fill with ice. Add lemonade. Garnish with a lemon wedge or wheel if desired.

Sometimes all you want is something simple like a vodka and lemonade. This drink has the same simplicity, but the ruby port adds more flavor and color without overpowering the the lemonade's refreshing summery taste. Mix a pitcher for a night on the patio with friends! Be sure to use ruby port, which is light on the palate and the wallet.

The Barstool Buzz:

"A perfect drink for amateurs to start with."

"Easy, neutral and smooth, with a nice finish."

"Refreshing and risky. I could down too many of these on a hot day."

B-52

½ ounce Kahlua
½ ounce Bailey's Irish cream
½ ounce Gran Marnier

Layer in shot glass.

With a little practice, you can layer a shot like a pro. You must pour in the order above so the liqueurs stay in layers. Pour in your first layer, then measure out the next in a jigger. Slide a small teaspoon into the glass with the backside facing up. Pour your next layer very slowly over the back of the spoon. Repeat. You may need a few friends to slam your mistakes until you get it just right!

The Barstool Buzz:

"Delicious coffee drink with a kick."

"Who could not like this combo?"

"Drop this bomb any time!"

Jack Rose

1½ ounces applejack brandy
½ ounce lemon juice
½ ounce grenadine

Combine with ice in a cocktail shaker.
Shake and strain into a cocktail glass.
Garnish with lemon twist if desired.

Any drink good enough
to make it into a
Hemingway novel
(*The Sun Also Rises*)
is good enough for
Thirsty Jane!
This Prohibition-era
delight probably got
its name from its main
ingredient, applejack and
its rose hue, although
some claim the drink
was named after a
1920s gangster.

The Barstool Buzz:

"Sweet apple balanced with tart lemon."

"I'll bet this comes out smelling like a rose."

"I hope a Jack Rose a day keeps the doctor away!"

Acknowledgements

So many people contributed to the birth of 3 Ingredient Cocktails, the first Thirsty Jane Guide, that thanking all of them would certainly exceed my allotted time and space. The biggest "thank you" goes to my husband and boozing partner, Paul. This book wouldn't exist without his inspiration and support. Second, perfecting each recipe was possible only with the help the neighborhood lushes who slogged through drink after drink, week after week, in my basement. I know they suffered at times! Toasts to Sarah and Doug who loaned me bar ware and to Joel who gave me access to his extensive cocktail book and bar ware collections. Finally, the creative team who worked on this book challenged me at every stage to make it the best. Lisarae gave each drink a sense of place and feeling in her magnificent photos. Walt put snap into my copy. Sally crossed all the t's and dotted the i's. And, Kim captured the Thirsty Jane vibe in the design and layout of the book. Thanks to you all — the next round's on me!

Who is Thirsty Jane?

Thisty Jane is J.K. O'Hanlon, a writer, jigger jockey, equal-opportunity-boozer and former corporate lawyer (perhaps the reason for the boozer epithet?). For J.K., nothing is more satisfying than handcrafting an exquisite cocktail for a friend and serving it in the perfect glass. Yet, when staring down six loads of laundry or entertaining the party of eight the hubby forgot to mention was coming over, she likes to reach for something simple and reliable, like all of the recipes in this book! When she's not mixing it up at home and/or slaving over a computer keyboard, J.K. enjoys making friends with bartenders around the world, wheedling out recipes and secrets whenever possible.